Robert Kirkwood

Illustrated by Edward McLachlan

 LONGMAN

To Mara

Contents

Introduction

LOOKING FOR PROOF OF GOD shares the same basic aims as the other two books in the series, **LOOKING FOR GOD** and **LOOKING FOR HAPPINESS**. These aims are:
a) to move away from the information orientation of Religious Studies to an exploration of the religious concerns of pupils;
b) to move away from the 'comparative religions' approach to focus on the PHILOSOPHY OF RELIGION – which not only has the advantage of being cross-cultural but also of dealing specifically with the sorts of questions pupils tend to ask about religion;
c) to meet some of the needs of MIXED-ABILITY TEACHING.

LOOKING FOR PROOF OF GOD has the specific aim of focusing attention on the issue of God's existence. It tries to do so by addressing itself to the question that pupils tend to ask whenever the issue is raised, i.e. 'Can you *prove* to me that God exists?'

This third book in the series examines firstly various historical attempts that have been made to provide evidence that would either *prove* or *disprove* God's existence. Secondly, it looks at what is generally agreed to be the ambiguous nature of this evidence. Finally, it tries to make clear how many religious and non-religious people make decisions about God's existence within this ambiguity. The book's conclusion is open-ended.

Robert Kirkwood

THE MAGICAL MYSTERY TOUR

These happy-looking tourists are being placed on the train by their tourist-guide. 'It's a magical mystery tour,' she is telling them, 'so don't ask me where you'll end up. You won't find that out until you arrive. For the time being just concentrate on enjoying the journey.'

The tourists attempted to do just that. They put all questions about the destination to the back of their minds. They put their bags in the racks, took off their coats and jackets, rolled up their sleeves, unpacked their picnic lunches, unplugged their flasks, sat back, put their feet up and prepared themselves for a relaxed and leisurely journey.

The journey, however, was to be neither relaxed nor leisurely. In fact, it turned out to be the sort of journey that made each of them 'sweat buckets' and wonder whether they would ever get off the train alive.

There were times, for example, when the train appeared to have no DRIVER, to be completely out of control and to be on the point of crashing and killing the lot of them. It would suddenly pick up speed like a roller-coaster at a fairground, hurtle down steep hills, fly round dangerous bends, crash through gates at level crossings, scream through narrow stations and completely ignore 'stop' signals and 'go slow' warning lights. The carriages, on these occasions, would rock wildly from side to side and life inside them for the tourists was not only uncomfortable but also extremely dangerous.

There were also times when the train appeared to have a DRIVER, to be under control and to be taking them safely to some as yet unknown destination. It would reduce its speed to a safe level, brake gently on steep hills, go slowly round dangerous bends, stop at level crossing gates, approach narrow stations with caution and observe 'stop' and 'go slow' warning lights. The carriages would rock gently from side to side and life inside for the tourists, on these occasions, would be comfortable, pleasant and safe.

The behaviour of the train was therefore **AMBIGUOUS**. On some occasions it suggested that there was a driver, while on others that there was not. The tourists were not sure what to believe about their 'mystery tour' or about their chances of surviving it.

That is why they are all sitting on the edges of their seats, biting their nails and looking petrified – instead of taking the advice of their tourist-guide. 'How can we possibly take her advice!' one said. 'How can we relax and enjoy the journey when the MYSTERY about this tour has turned out to be whether there's a DRIVER and whether we are all going to end up dead?'

Many people today say that the situation facing these tourists is the same sort of situation that is facing all human beings.

Well, first of all, they point out that all human beings whether they like it or not are also taking part in a mystery journey. This journey, they say, is the JOURNEY OF LIFE itself and takes place not on a train or through countryside but on *this world* and through the *passage of time*.

Secondly, they point out that many people will give you the same sort of advice as the guide gave the tourists – as you set out on this 'journey of life'. They will tell you not to think too much, or ask too many questions about where the 'journey of life' is going. 'Nobody knows where you'll end up,' they say. 'You'll only find that out when you arrive. You should concentrate on simply having a good time while the journey lasts.'

Finally, they say that – once again like the tourists – this sort of advice is difficult to take because 'the world' on which our journey takes place behaves just as AMBIGUOUSLY as the tourists' train. There are times when the world's behaviour is so chaotic that it seems as if the 'driver' we call GOD doesn't actually exist and that our journey is out of control and moving simply by chance.

There are other occasions, however, when the opposite is true and the world's behaviour seems so orderly that the evidence points to this GOD existing. Like the tourists then the 'mystery' of our journey also turns out to be whether or not there is a **driver** (GOD) and whether we are going to arrive safely or going to end up dead.

1 It is important that you understand the meaning of the word AMBIGUOUS because it is used in every chapter of this book.
   (a) Look up the meaning of this word in a dictionary.
   (b) Write out two sentences with this word included to show that you understand its meaning.
   (c) Explain what this sentence means: 'The behaviour of the train was AMBIGUOUS.' (page 7)

2 In this chapter it was stated that all human beings face the same sort of problems as the tourists on the train. In your own words explain what this means.

3 Whatever your beliefs about GOD might be try to write down:
   (a) A list of evidence for GOD's existence.
   (b) A list of evidence against GOD's existence.

4 Many people think that GOD's existence would be *proved* if He showed Himself in a vision. If you were to see a vision of a person claiming to be GOD would this be proof for you? Give reasons for your answer.

5 Is there any sort of evidence that would definitely *prove* to you that GOD either exists or doesn't exist. Give reasons for your answer.

'I CAN PROVE THAT GOD EXISTS'

This is a picture of a man called **St Thomas Aquinas**. He was born in Italy at a place called Roccasecca in 1224. He died in 1274. St Thomas Aquinas was a **philosopher** and a **theologian**. He had no doubt whatsoever that there was a GOD guiding the 'journey of life'. The evidence for His existence, St Thomas thought, was clear. It is so clear, he said, that if you only think about the evidence sensibly you will see that it actually **proves** that **GOD EXISTS**. He was so sure that this was the case that he wrote a book in which he expounded '**five proofs for the existence of GOD**'.

In this chapter we are going to examine one of these 'proofs'.

THE FIRST CAUSE

'The most important piece of evidence to be examined,' said St Thomas Aquinas, 'is the fact that "The Universe" actually exists.' He suggested that you should begin your examination of the evidence by looking at 'The Universe' and asking yourself this simple question:

HOW DID THE UNIVERSE GET HERE?

'You know, of course,' said St Thomas, 'that the Universe couldn't have simply sprung from NOTHING. Some-THING just cannot come out of no-THING. This theory doesn't make any sort of sense.' Therefore you are forced by your own **reason** to the conclusion that 'The Universe' was **caused** to exist by something that existed before it.

But we <u>know</u> what existed before the Universe and caused it to exist.... It was a BIG BANG!

If St Thomas Aquinas were alive today he would not agree, however, that this BIG BANG is an answer to the question 'HOW DID THE UNIVERSE GET HERE?'

St Thomas would say that it cannot be an answer because you now need to explain what it was that **caused** the BIG BANG to take place and also what it was that **caused the cause of the BIG BANG**.

That is what St Thomas thought as well. He said that it does not make sense to keep on asking this question without ever coming to a conclusion. Our minds tell us that it makes more sense to believe that all of these **causes** must have had a beginning.

Once again, said St Thomas, we are forced by REASON to accept that the only sensible explanation is that there must have been a **first cause** that was UNCAUSED by anything else existing before it. This 'first cause', said St Thomas, can only be GOD.

1 St Thomas Aquinas said that if we want to *prove* to ourselves that GOD exists then we should begin by asking ourselves a simple question. What is this question?

2 Some people try to answer this question by talking about a 'Big Bang'.
   (a) Explain what this 'Big Bang' is supposed to have done.
   (b) Explain why St Thomas would have said that this cannot be an answer to *the question*.

3 St Thomas said that *this question* can only be answered by talking about a 'first cause'.
   (a) Explain what he thought this 'first cause' was.
   (b) Explain why he thought that the 'first cause' was the only sensible answer.
   (c) Do you agree with St Thomas? Give reasons for your answer.

HAS HE PROVED ANYTHING?

When a person *proves* a particular theory to be correct it means that they have gathered together enough evidence to force any reasonable person to accept it as the truth. St Thomas was claiming to have this sort of PROOF.

Many people today, however, say that this is not the case. They claim that you can look at St Thomas Aquinas' evidence and actually come away with the sensible conclusion that GOD **doesn't** exist.

These people often explain how this is possible by first agreeing with St Thomas that the 'Universe' must have been CAUSED to exist by something that existed before it. They also agree that you therefore need to set up a **chain reaction of causes** to explain the CAUSE OF THE CAUSE OF THE CAUSE etc.

They say, however, that there is no reason on earth why anybody has to agree with St Thomas that all of these CAUSES must have started somewhere and that the only sensible explanation is that there must have been a 'first cause' i.e. GOD. It makes just as much sense, they say, to believe that the chain reaction of causes stretches endlessly backwards. That, in fact, it has no beginning at all.

These people don't agree that St Thomas has managed to *prove* that GOD exists. His evidence, they say, is **AMBIGUOUS**. You can look at it and sensibly come to the conclusion that either GOD exists or that He doesn't exist. The question whether or not there is a DRIVER guiding the 'journey of life' must, they say, remain an open question.

---

1 Many people today say that St Thomas Aquinas hasn't proved that GOD exists. They say that you can explain the existence of the 'Universe' without talking about a 'first cause'.
   (a) What alternative explanation do they give?
   (b) Can you think of any other explanation?

2 This chapter has suggested that both the *FIRST CAUSE* explanation and the *ENDLESS CHAIN REACTION* explanation are both **possible**. Which explanation do you think is most **probable**? Give reasons for your answer.

3 **Research**
   Read Genesis chapter 1. Does this text agree more with St Thomas Aquinas or those who disagree with him? Give reasons for your answer.

'I CAN PROVE THAT GOD DOESN'T EXIST'

This is a picture of **Ludwig Feuerbach**. He was born in Germany in 1804 and died in 1872. He – like St Thomas Aquinas – spent many years of his life studying books on THEOLOGY and PHILOSOPHY. Unlike St Thomas, however, his studies led him to the conclusion that there is no GOD guiding the 'journey of life'. His reasons for coming to this conclusion can be summed up in two of his own sentences:

'WHAT MAN IS IN **NEED OF** HE MAKES HIS GOD.'

'WHAT MAN **WISHES TO BE** HE MAKES HIS GOD.'

This chapter will be trying to explain what these two sentences mean.

IMAGINE THAT

All human beings want to be **happy**, said Feuerbach. The problem is that we all find it difficult to be happy on the 'journey of life'. We fear that it may be a journey with no GOD in control and so no destination other than the grave. A journey then which we cannot survive and which will end in our total extinction from the 'Universe'.

So terrible is the thought that there is no GOD, said Feuerbach, that our **IMAGINATION** steps in and creates one for us. The GOD that we all so desperately need in order to be *happy*, we simply invent ourselves and imagine to be real. *'WHAT MAN IS IN NEED OF* (then) *HE MAKES HIS GOD.'*

Human imagination doesn't simply imagine any sort of God, said Feuerbach. It is careful to create for us a GOD with a **personality** that can be **trusted** to bring us to the end of our journey alive and well.

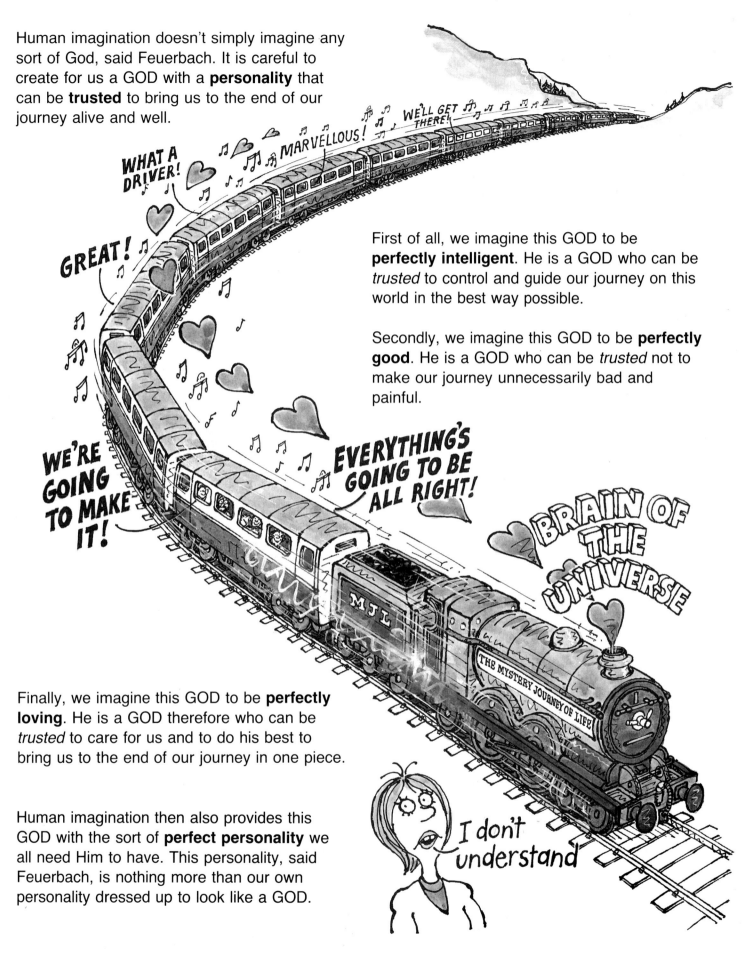

First of all, we imagine this GOD to be **perfectly intelligent**. He is a GOD who can be *trusted* to control and guide our journey on this world in the best way possible.

Secondly, we imagine this GOD to be **perfectly good**. He is a GOD who can be *trusted* not to make our journey unnecessarily bad and painful.

Finally, we imagine this GOD to be **perfectly loving**. He is a GOD therefore who can be *trusted* to care for us and to do his best to bring us to the end of our journey in one piece.

Human imagination then also provides this GOD with the sort of **perfect personality** we all need Him to have. This personality, said Feuerbach, is nothing more than our own personality dressed up to look like a GOD.

Feuerbach said that what human imagination does is act like a projector in a cinema. It projects into Heaven an imaginary picture of GOD. Then it projects into this GOD a picture of our own **human intelligence, goodness** and **love** with all the imperfections filtered out – a glamourised picture of our own human personality as we would ideally like it to be.

'GOD is no more than a projection of man (ourselves),' said Feuerbach. When believers worship Him they are simply bowing down and worshipping an ideal picture of themselves. '*WHAT MAN WISHES TO BE* (then) *HE MAKES HIS GOD.*'

1 There seems to be little doubt that our imagination does attempt, on occasions, to make us happy. Sometimes, for example, we *imagine* that a particular boy or girl likes us a lot and perhaps even wants to go out with us, when in fact they can't stand the sight of us. Give examples from your own life when your imagination has stepped in and imagined that something is *real* in order to make you happy.

2 In your own words explain what Ludwig Feuerbach means when he says that 'WHAT MAN IS IN NEED OF HE MAKES HIS GOD'.

3 Many people say that the sorts of things we imagine can tell us a lot about our (secret) selves. For example, look at the inkblots below. Examine them carefully.

(a) Write down the thing(s) you imagine you can see in the shapes.

(b) Compare your results with those of the person sitting next to you and try to explain why you imagined different things (if that is the case).

(c) Do you think that what you imagined you saw in the inkblots can tell us anything about some of your (secret) wishes? In other words, are they a *projection of some part of yourself?* Give reasons for your answer.

4 Explain in your own words what Feuerbach means when he says 'WHAT MAN WISHES TO BE HE MAKES HIS GOD'.

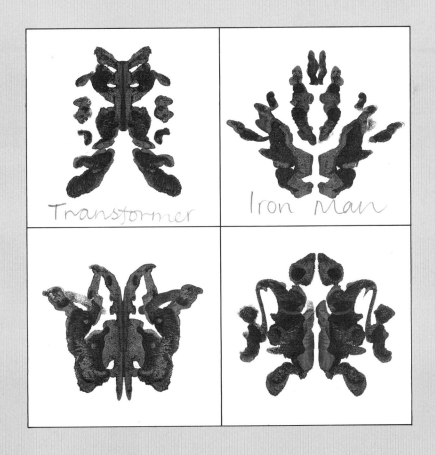

HAS <u>HE</u> PROVED ANYTHING?

If Ludwig Feuerbach has managed to 'prove' that GOD doesn't exist then once again there should be no way of looking at his 'evidence' and coming to any other conclusion. Many people, however, say that this isn't the case. They say that you can look at Feuerbach's 'evidence' and still come away with a sensible belief in GOD.

But his evidence seems so strong....

How can anybody do that?

What these people are saying is that even if it is true that we IMAGINE GOD's existence it does not follow from this that GOD is not **real**.

WE DON'T UNDERSTAND WHAT YOU MEAN!

Look at this boy. He has come to the conclusion that he will only be really HAPPY if he can meet and marry a particular sort of girl. What he does then is to IMAGINE that this sort of girl exists somewhere in the world.

It doesn't follow, of course, that this girl **actually exists** just because he IMAGINES that she does. He may spend his life with this imaginary picture and never actually meet such a person.

It also does not follow that this girl **doesn't exist** just because he IMAGINES that she does. He may actually meet and marry such a person (the girl of his dreams) and so discover that what he imagined existed, actually did.

These people say that this is also true of GOD. In other words, it doesn't follow that GOD **actually exists** just because you IMAGINE that He does. Neither does it follow that GOD **doesn't exist** just because you IMAGINED it to be so. Imagination, they point out, neither *proves nor disproves* the existence of GOD.

Such people do not agree that Feuerbach has managed to 'prove' that GOD doesn't exist. They say that his evidence is as AMBIGUOUS as the evidence of St Thomas Aquinas. You can look at it and sensibly come to the conclusion that either GOD exists or that He doesn't exist. The question whether or not there is a DRIVER guiding the 'journey of life' must once again, they say, remain an open question.

1 Many people say that Ludwig Feuerbach hasn't 'proved' that GOD doesn't exist. They say that *imagination neither proves nor disproves the existence of GOD.* In your own words, explain what they mean.

2 Try to think of occasions when you IMAGINED that something was 'real' and when your imagination was also telling you the truth.

3 Ludwig Feuerbach may not have 'proved' that God doesn't exist. Do you think, however, that what he has said is *probably* the truth? Give reasons for your answer.

4 A man called Karl Marx (who borrowed a lot of Feuerbach's ideas) also said that GOD doesn't exist. 'RELIGION,' he argued, 'IS THE OPIUM OF THE MASSES.'

Marx → communism

(a) Explain what you think he means by this.

(b) Think about the way Feuerbach has been criticised in this chapter. Could Karl Marx be criticised in a similar sort of way?

5 Some people say that:

'**Atheism** is a projection of man's imagination.'

'**Atheism** is the opium of the intellectuals.'

(a) What do you think these phrases mean?

(b) Do you agree? Give reasons for your answers.

'I CAN ALSO PROVE THAT GOD EXISTS'

This is a picture of a man called **William Paley**. He was born in 1743 and died in 1805. Like St Thomas Aquinas he was also convinced that the evidence pointed overwhelmingly to there being a DRIVER called GOD guiding the 'journey of life'. Like St Thomas, he tried to show that this was the case by writing out an argument which he thought would *prove* that GOD exists. This argument is known as **THE TELEOLOGICAL ARGUMENT** (or the argument of DESIGN and PURPOSE) and this chapter examines it.

THE TELEOLOGICAL ARGUMENT

William Paley suggested that you should imagine walking across open countryside with some friends and suddenly coming across a watch hidden amongst the grass. You pick up the watch and are so impressed by its craftwork that you ask your friends: 'WHO DO YOU THINK MADE THIS?'

The design of the watch is more complicated than what's in his head!

Now imagine, said William Paley, that one of your friends replies: 'Nobody actually made the watch. It has always existed and has always been there.'

If a friend were to give you this sort of reply, said Paley, you would naturally be entitled to think that he/she had not seen the object clearly or that he/she had but were not wired up properly.

The reason is obvious, said Paley. The watch simply shows too much evidence of DESIGN and PURPOSE for nobody to have been responsible for its existence.

'We see a cylindrical box containing a coiled elastic spring, which, by its endeavour to relax itself, turns round the box. We next observe a flexible chain communicating the action of the spring from the box to the fusee. We then find a series of wheels, the teeth of which catch in, and apply to, each other, conducting the motion from the fusee to the balance and from the balance to the pointer, and at the same time, by the size and shape of those wheels, so regulating that motion as to terminate in causing an index, by an equable and measured progression, to pass over a given space in a given time. We take notice that the wheels are made of brass in order to keep them from rust; the springs of steel, no other metal being so elastic; that over the face of the watch there is placed a glass, a material employed in no other part of the work, but in the room of which, if there had been any other than a transparent substance, the hour could not be seen without opening the case. This mechanism being observed, the inference, we think is *inevitable*, that the watch must have had a maker.'

William Paley, *Natural Theology* (1802)

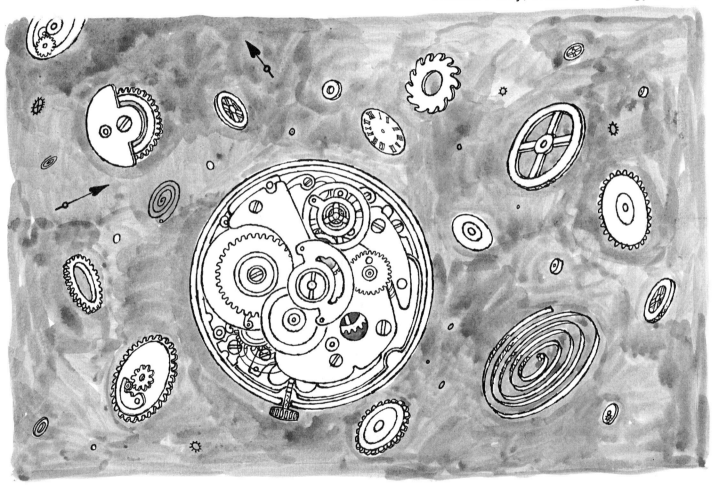

There is then, said Paley, only one possible sensible answer to the question 'WHO DO YOU THINK MADE THIS?' and that is to give the name of a person who has a skilled **designing mind**. We reach this conclusion because if any object shows evidence of DESIGN and PURPOSE then the inference is inevitable – there must be a **maker**.

William Paley continued his argument by saying that if it is nonsense to say that a watch came about by chance or has always existed then it is equally nonsensical to say that the 'Universe' came about by chance or has always existed. He argued that the 'Universe' (like the watch) shows evidence of too much complicated DESIGN and PURPOSE for that to be the case.

Consider, for example, the complicated body-designs of animals, birds and fish. Think how each is so perfectly **designed** for life on the land, sea and air. Or consider, in particular, the DESIGN of your own **eyes, ears** and **nose** and how once again they are each so perfectly **designed** to fulfil the PURPOSE of **seeing, hearing** and **smelling**.

There is then, said William Paley, only one sensible answer that can be given to the question 'WHO or WHAT made the Universe?' and that is to say that because it shows so much evidence of DESIGN and PURPOSE it must therefore have been **designed** by **a designer** i.e. GOD:

1 Explain in your own words how William Paley uses the DESIGN and PURPOSE of a watch to try to prove the existence of GOD.

2 Do you agree with William Paley's argument? Give reasons for your answer. Perhaps in your answer you could discuss the following:

(a) Is Paley right to compare a *watch* to the 'Universe'?

(b) Has Paley made it clear what the PURPOSE of the 'Universe' is (as he did with the watch)?

3 Read Psalm 104 and explain why the writer of this psalm would probably have supported the views of William Paley.

HAS HE SUCCEEDED?

If William Paley has managed to prove that GOD exists, once again there should be no way of looking at 'the evidence' and coming to any other conclusion. Many people, however, say that – like the proofs of Aquinas and Feuerbach – this just is not the case. In fact, you can look at Paley's 'evidence' and come to the conclusion that GOD doesn't exist.

HOW COME?

Well, you could, for example, agree with William Paley that the 'Universe' contains ORDER and that this order is necessary for life to begin and survive.

I STILL don't understand what you're getting at...

You do not have to agree, however, that this ORDER was designed by a designing mind called GOD. You could say that this ORDER is simply the product of chance.

Imagine being given two dice and told to keep throwing these dice until all the possible combinations of numbers come up. Sooner or later (given enough time) you will achieve the task.

What is being said is that NATURE is playing a similar game. Instead of throwing dice it is throwing atoms around and because it has INFINITE-TIME to play then these atoms will sooner or later go through all their possible combinations. The order that you see then in the 'Universe' is not designed-order; it is simply the result of one of Nature's many throws with the atoms. The ORDER is simply the result of **chance** and not a DESIGNING GOD.

These people then do not agree that William Paley has 'proved' that GOD exists. They say that his evidence (as with the evidence put forward by Aquinas and Feuerbach) is AMBIGUOUS. You can look at it and sensibly come to the conclusion that either GOD exists or that He doesn't exist. Once again the question whether or not there is a DRIVER guiding the 'journey of life' must remain an open question.

---

1 (a) Many people believe that the 'Universe' contains *order*. They do not necessarily believe that this order was *designed* by GOD. Explain how they think this *order* came about (as explained in this chapter).

(b) Can you think of an alternative explanation for this *order*?

2 (a) There are people who just cannot accept that a GOD designed the 'Universe'. 'The world', they say, is full of too much suffering for that to be the case. Read the following extract and in your own words explain how this religious writer would reply to these people.

Human freedom involves the risk of error and of suffering but it is essential to humanity. Without it we would be different creatures. God could indeed have made the world one in which there could be no pain and no sin. But that would not have been an improved version of the world we know. It would have been a totally different world . . .

In the best world possible there must be the risk of suffering. But this is a testimony to God's love, not a denial of it. It is not because he does not love us but because he does, that God has made the world one in which suffering may occur.

Let us suppose that I have a child just coming to the toddling stage and that I love him. When he comes to the point of taking his first steps on his own, what do I do? I have the power to prevent his walking on his own, and since I love him, I do not want him to fall and be hurt. But, since I love him, I also want him to learn to walk. I know that he must, or else he will not, cannot, grow into the complete man I want him to be. I therefore permit him to walk on his own with all the attendant risk of sustaining hurt. I permit that risk, not because I do not love my child, but because I do.

It is in a way not altogether dissimilar to this that, for love of us, God must restrain himself and allow the possibility of suffering in this world.

James Martin, *Suffering Man, Loving God* (Collins)

(b) Do you agree with this writer's reply? Give reasons for your answer.

3 It is possible that GOD did **design** the 'Universe' and also possible that He didn't. Which do you believe is *probable*? Give reasons.

IT'S ALL A GAMBLE

This is a picture of **Blaise Pascal**. He was born in France in 1623 and died at the age of 39. He was a genius. At the age of 16 he was one of the leading mathematicians of his day. He was also a brilliant physicist (he invented the hydraulic press) and a brilliant engineer (he invented the first calculating machine).

When Pascal applied his brain-power to the problem of whether or not GOD existed, his conclusion was very different to those of Aquinas, Feuerbach and Paley. GOD's existence, he said, can be neither proved nor disproved. Whatever you decide about this problem will be uncertain. Your answer can be nothing more than a (calculated) **gamble**. There are, however, two points to consider said Pascal before placing your bet. This chapter will be looking at what these two points are.

YOU MUST GAMBLE

Blaise Pascal said that you should understand, first of all, that there is no way you can avoid making a gamble on GOD either existing or not existing. You have to place your bet whether you like it or not. It is one of the conditions of life. It is not like gambling on cards or horses. You can, if you so choose, live in this world without making these sorts of gambles. You must, however, make a gamble on GOD.
A choice is inevitable for you either choose '**to live in this world as if GOD exists**' or you choose '**to live in this world as if He doesn't exist**'.

Why should I _have_ to gamble? —I could just say I don't know if **GOD** exists or not, so I'm not going to make any choice.

No choice is a choice, said Pascal. If you say 'I don't know and so can't choose whether GOD exists or doesn't exist' then you actually end up LIVING IN THIS WORLD AS IF HE DOESN'T EXIST. So there are only two choices: **GOD IS** or **GOD IS NOT**. 'Come then,' said Pascal, 'what will you wager?'

Pascal said you will probably be helped to decide if you also understand that there is actually only one way to WIN ANYTHING in this gamble.

Just consider what you stand to GAIN or LOSE by betting against GOD existing.

If you are wrong and GOD exists then you stand to lose a great deal. For a start you will **lose** the HAPPINESS that is possible during the 'journey of life' believing that there is a 'driver' and that He is taking you to a destination beyond the grave. You will probably also have to face the judgement of GOD and so lose the HAPPINESS of eternal life in Heaven.

If you are right however and GOD doesn't exist, you don't actually **gain** anything. Life, as you predicted, is 'driverless' and is therefore a journey to the grave. You simply end up dead. You don't even have the satisfaction of saying to yourself or others that you were right because *you* won't be around anyway.

Now consider what you stand to GAIN or LOSE by betting for GOD existing.

If you are wrong and GOD doesn't exist then you don't actually stand to **lose** anything at all. You will simply end up dead (as you would do if you gambled against HIM existing and were right). You won't even have to suffer the humiliation of being wrong because once again *you* won't be around and neither will anybody else.

If however you are right and GOD exists, 'then,' said Pascal, 'you will have gained in all possible ways. First of all you will have **gained HAPPINESS** during the "journey of life" believing that there was a "driver" and secondly you will also gain eternal HAPPINESS IN HEAVEN.'

We've chosen to live our lives as if God exists!

There is then only one sensible choice to make, said Pascal. LIVE IN THIS WORLD AS IF GOD DOES EXIST, for unlike betting against Him, you **lose nothing** if you are wrong and **gain everything** if you are right.

1 Explain why Blaise Pascal thought that making a decision about God's existence can only be a *gamble*.

2 (a) Pascal said that no human being could escape gambling on God's existence. Explain why.
  (b) Do you agree? Give reasons for your answer.

3 (a) Pascal also said that everybody should gamble on God existing rather than not existing. Explain in your own words why he said this.
  (b) Do you agree? Give reasons for your answer.

4 Pascal seems to give the impression that you can *choose* to believe what you want. Can you? (Give examples of choices to support your answer.)

IS PASCAL RIGHT?
IS PROOF IMPOSSIBLE?

Many people today (both religious and non-religious) agree with Blaise Pascal that human beings will never be able to **prove** the existence or non-existence of a being called GOD. 'This will always be impossible,' they say, 'because the human mind relies too much on the **five senses** to give it the proof it is looking for.' The five senses, however, are limited. They can only provide proof of beings existing or not existing who in principle are made of atoms. In other words, proof of beings, like human beings, who we can SEE, HEAR, TOUCH, TASTE and SMELL.

I have no doubt whatsoever that THIS person exists!

They point out that if such a being as GOD exists it is not going to be made of atoms. GOD is going to be, as many religious people say, a **non-material, invisible, spiritual being** who doesn't simply exist outside of us but who also exists within us as well.

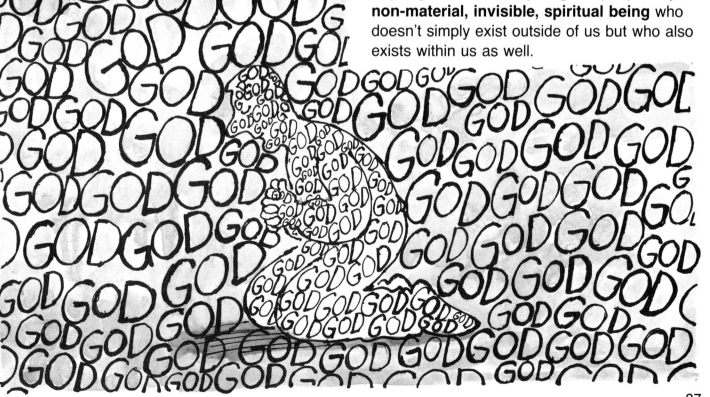

Many would say then that trying to PROVE the existence or non-existence of a **spiritual being** called GOD with the human mind is like trying to PROVE the existence or non-existence of water with a metal detector.

I CAN'T DETECT IT WITH THIS MACHINE SO I DON'T BELIEVE IN WATER!

I CAN'T SEE HIM WITH THIS TELESCOPE SO I DON'T BELIEVE IN GOD!

In other words the human mind, like the metal detector, is simply the wrong tool for the job.

Well, if you can't prove God's existence then Pascal was right....It can only be a gamble whether he exists or not.

Many people, both religious and non-religious, disagree with Pascal and say that if you are an honest person then making decisions about GOD's existence cannot be like gambling on the horses. When you gamble, they point out, your choice is generally guided by your chance of **gaining** or **winning** something for yourself.

However, when you are trying to make honest decisions about GOD either existing or not existing then, they say, your choice cannot be guided by what you might profit. You can only be guided by what you have decided is 'the truth', whatever the **gain** or **loss** might be.

1 (a) Many people say that trying to prove the existence of God with the human mind is like trying to prove the existence of water with a metal detector. Explain why.

(b) Do you agree? Give reasons.

2 (a) Many say that Pascal is wrong to compare decisions about God's existence to gambling. Explain why.

(b) Do you agree? Give reasons for your answer.

3 Can you think of things you are 'certain' of but which you cannot *prove* or *disprove* with the human mind. If you can, give examples. If you can't, explain why not.

TO TRUST OR NOT TO TRUST

Religious people throughout the world may tell you that they have decided that GOD exists, that He is controlling the journey of life and that they will end up somewhere safe when their journey on this world has come to an end. We have made this decision, they say, not because the 'available evidence' proves His existence but rather because this evidence makes His existence so PROBABLE that we are able to **trust** that He is there. This **act of trust** is MORE REASONABLE than not trusting.

So belief in GOD rests on nothing more than *TRUST!*

DECISIONS

You should not be surprised that religious people base their choice on REASONABLE TRUST rather than on PROOF. Most decisions that we all make are, in fact, just like this: they have to be because most of the time we have no way of **proving in advance** which choice is correct. Look at these examples:

In each of the situations shown on page 41 – which are very typical of life – there are people who have to make a choice. There is no possibility of being able to **prove in advance** what will be the right choice to make. A decision must then be made between uncertain choices. They could, of course, simply flip a coin to decide. However, most people in these sorts of situations don't do this. Instead they look at the 'available evidence' and then decide – like people making decisions about GOD – whether it is more reasonable TO TRUST or NOT TO TRUST.

1 Explain the difference between making a decision based on *proof* and making a decision based on *reasonable trust*.

2 Imagine you are the person who has to make the decision in each of the three examples on page 41. Explain the sort of evidence you would be looking for in each case. Make a list.

3 Try to think of occasions in your own life when you have had to decide whether TO TRUST or NOT TO TRUST. Give examples of the evidence you had to consider. Also explain what decision you made.

One writer has tried to explain the religious person's ACT OF TRUST in this parable:

THE STRANGER

In time of war in an occupied country, a member of the resistance meets one night a stranger who deeply impresses him. They spend that night together in conversation. The Stranger tells the partisan that he is himself on the side of the resistance – indeed that he is in command of it, and urges the partisan to have faith in him no matter what happens. The partisan is utterly convinced at that meeting of the Stranger's sincerity and constancy and undertakes to trust him.

They never meet in conditions of intimacy again. But sometimes the Stranger is seen helping members of the resistance, and the partisan is grateful and says to his friends, 'He is on our side.'

Sometimes he is seen in the uniform of the police handing over patriots to the occupying power. On these occasions his friends murmur against him: but the partisan still says, 'He is on our side.' He still believes that, in spite of appearances, the Stranger did not deceive him. Sometimes he asks the Stranger for help and receives it. He is then thankful. Sometimes he asks and does not receive it. Then he says, 'The Stranger knows best.' Sometimes his friends, in exasperation, say, 'Well, what would he have to do for you to admit that you were wrong and that he is not on our side?' But the partisan refuses to answer. He will not consent to put the Stranger to the test. And sometimes his friends complain: 'Well, if that's what you mean by his being on our side, the sooner he goes over to the other side the better.'

The partisan of the parable does not allow anything to count decisively against the proposition 'The Stranger is on our side.' This is because he has committed himself to trust the Stranger. But he of course recognises that the Stranger's **ambiguous** behaviour does count against what he believes about him. It is precisely this situation which constitutes the trial of his faith.

Basil Mitchell

From *New Essays in Philosophical Theology*, Eds Flew and McIntyre (SCM Press, 1955)

The writer of this parable is saying that all human beings are in the same sort of situation as the partisans. When we are born into our world, whether we like it or not, we all come face to face with a 'Universe' that is both **strange** and **mysterious**. This strange 'Universe' also acts just as AMBIGUOUSLY as the Stranger in the parable.

There are times, for example, when the 'Universe' appears to be under the control of a loving personality known as GOD. On these occasions the 'Universe' appears to care about us, to value our lives, to be concerned about our safety and so to be most certainly 'on our side'.

There are other times, however, when the opposite appears to be true – when no loving personality called GOD seems to be in control of the behaviour of the 'Universe'. On these occasions the 'Universe' appears not to care about us, not to value our lives, to be coldly and impersonally unconcerned about our safety and so to be very much 'against us'.

Like the partisans, we must make a decision therefore in which our very existence is at stake for we must also decide whether the stranger we meet (which is the 'Universe') is '**on our side**' or '**against us**'.

The writer is also saying that religious people are those who act like the main partisan in the story. They are people who accept that 'the evidence' is AMBIGUOUS but who are nevertheless convinced that 'the evidence' taken as a whole gives more support to GOD's existence than to His non-existence.

O thou who art at home
Deep in my heart
Enable me to join you
Deep in my heart.

(*from a song of the Talmud*)

Religious people then are those who are willing to commit themselves to **trusting** that GOD is REAL and that our strange 'Universe', in spite sometimes of appearances, is therefore 'on our side'. Such an ACT OF TRUST, they say, is more reasonable than not trusting.

1 Explain why religious people say that all human beings are in the same sort of situation as the partisan who met the Stranger. In your answer explain:
   (a) which *stranger* we meet;
   (b) how our *stranger* acts like the Stranger in the parable;
   (c) what decision we have to make.

2 (a) Explain why religious people are like the partisan *who met* the Stranger.
   (b) Why are atheists and agnostics like the other partisans in the parable?

REASONABLE TRUST

Well, if you can only <u>trust</u> that **GOD** exists, that means you can never be certain that he's real.

I DON'T UNDERSTAND

Religious people disagree. They say that this ACT OF REASONABLE TRUST goes on to make them more and more **certain** that GOD IS REAL. They often explain how by comparing their **certainty** with the way in which you can be **certain** that somebody loves you.

Look at this girl. She is very anxious because she is not *certain* that her boyfriend is telling her the truth when he says 'I love you'. She spends a great deal of time testing him and trying to PROVE that his love is real. The results of the tests though are always AMBIGUOUS. She just cannot find the sort of CERTAINTY that will give her the peace of mind she is looking for.

I can't come out tonight, John, I've got to stay in and watch some paint dry...

Many would say that the only way that this girl will ever be *certain* that her boyfriend is telling the truth is if she stops being suspicious and learns to trust that his love exists. When she takes this '**act of reasonable trust**' she will experience her boyfriend's love and it will be this **experience** (and *not* PROOF) that will give her the 'certainty' she is looking for.

Religious people claim that their ACT OF TRUST gives them the same sort of 'certainty'. We cannot *prove* that GOD is real, they say, but by trusting we open ourselves to a direct **EXPERIENCE OF GOD**. It is by this overwhelming experience that we become increasingly certain that GOD IS REAL, that He is controlling the 'journey of life' and that we are going to arrive somewhere safely.

O thou who art at home
Deep in my heart
Let me lose myself in thee
Deep in my heart.

(*from a song of the Talmud*)

1 Make a list of the different methods used by some people to try to *prove* that somebody *loves* them.

2 Do you think that any of these methods can give *proof*? Give reasons for your answer.

3 This chapter has suggested that there is only one way you can be more and more certain that somebody loves you.
(a) Explain how.
(b) Do you agree? Give reasons.

4 The expression *'more and more certain'* is meant to suggest that 'certainty' is something which grows and must continually overcome doubts. Do you agree? Give reasons for your answer.

5 Religious people also say that they can become *more and more* certain that GOD exists.
(a) Explain how.
(b) Why do you think that religious people say that they become *'more and more'* certain that God exists? (Look at question 4.)

6 (a) Religious people often describe their *experience* of GOD as the experience of a **presence** – of not feeling alone in this world. Read, for example, this extract written by a modern day religious writer called Carlo Carretto:

> I don't know how it happened to you, but I know how it happened to me.
> God arrived in my heart like a huge parable. Everything around me spoke to me of Him.
>
> The sky spoke to me of Him,
> the earth spoke to me of Him,
> the sea spoke to me of Him.
> He was like a secret hidden in all things, visible and invisible.
> He was like the solution to all problems.
> He was like the most important Person who had ever entered my life and with whom I should have lived for ever.
> Very soon I felt myself enveloped by Him as a 'Presence always Present', one who looked at me from all the leaves of the wood I was walking through, and across the clouds riding briskly along the sky above my head.
> I have never had any difficulty in feeling God's presence, especially when I was small. Rather, His absence would have seemed very strange and very unlikely.
> I felt myself to be in God
> like a bird in the air
> like a log in the fire
> like a baby in its mother's womb.
> This last image was the strongest, the truest, and it is always growing.
> I truly think that a woman's womb containing a baby is the theme of the whole universe, the visibility of invisible things, the sign of the way God works in order to make me His son.
> In Him I live and breathe, and I rejoice in His Presence as creator, even if – and I suffer for it – the time has not yet come for me to see his divine countenance, as the Bible says, 'face to face' (I Corinthians 13: 12).
> It is early yet.
>
> *The Desert in the City* (Collins, 1979)

(b) Turn to Psalm 139: 1–12 in the Bible and read how another religious writer, who lived over 2000 years ago, describes the same experience. Do you think that this writer's *experience of GOD* is similar to that of Carlo Carretto? Give reasons for your answer.

7 Now try to explain what your *experience* of life is like.
(a) Do you, like these writers, sometimes (or always) experience the presence of GOD?
(b) Or is your experience one of being alone in this 'Universe'?

8 Read John 20: 19–29. What do you think Jesus meant in verse 29?